20 best
slow cooker
dinner recipes

Houghton Mifflin Harcourt
Boston • New York • 2013

Copyright © 2013 by General Mills, Minneapolis, Minnesota. All rights reserved.

Yoplait is a registered trademark of YOPLAIT MARQUES (France) used under license.

For information about permission to reproduce selections from this book, write to Permissions, Houghton Mifflin Harcourt Publishing Company, 215 Park Avenue South, New York, New York 10003.

www.hmhco.com

Cover photo: Family-Favorite Chili (page 23)

General Mills
Food Content and Relationship Marketing Director: Geoff Johnson
Food Content Marketing Manager: Susan Klobuchar
Senior Editor: Grace Wells
Kitchen Manager: Ann Stuart
Recipe Development and Testing: Betty Crocker Kitchens
Photography: General Mills Photography Studios and Image Library

Houghton Mifflin Harcourt
Publisher: Natalie Chapman
Editorial Director: Cindy Kitchel
Executive Editor: Anne Ficklen
Associate Editor: Heather Dabah
Managing Editor: Rebecca Springer
Production Editor: Kristi Hart
Cover Design: Chrissy Kurpeski
Book Design: Tai Blanche

ISBN 978-0-544-31484-9
Printed in the United States of America

The Betty Crocker Kitchens seal guarantees success in your kitchen. Every recipe has been tested in America's Most Trusted Kitchens™ to meet our high standards of reliability, easy preparation and great taste.

FIND MORE GREAT IDEAS AT
BettyCrocker.com

Dear Friends,

This new collection of colorful mini books has been put together with you in mind because we know that you love great recipes and enjoy cooking and baking but have a busy lifestyle. So every little book in the series contains just 20 recipes for you to treasure and enjoy. Plus, each book is a single subject designed in a bite-size format just for you—it's easy to use and is filled with favorite recipes from the Betty Crocker Kitchens!

All of the books are conveniently divided into short chapters so you can quickly find what you're looking for, and the beautiful photos throughout are sure to entice you into making the delicious recipes. In the series, you'll discover a fabulous array of recipes to spark your interest—from cookies, cupcakes and birthday cakes to party ideas for a variety of occasions. There's grilled foods, potluck favorites and even gluten-free recipes too.

You'll love the variety in these mini books—so pick one or choose them all for your cooking pleasure.

Enjoy and happy cooking!

Sincerely,

Betty Crocker

contents

Family Favorites
Beef and Potatoes with Rosemary • 6
Cheeseburger Joes • 7
Porketta Pot Roast • 8
Pulled Jerk Pork Sandwiches • 9
Chicken and Vegetables with
    Dumplings • 10
Tuscan Turkey and Beans • 11
Jambalaya • 12

Global Flavors
Chunky Beef Ragu • 13
Carnitas • 14
German Red Cabbage and Pork Ribs • 15
Mediterranean Chicken Marbella • 16
Spicy Chicken in Peanut Sauce • 17
Vegetable Curry with Couscous • 18

Satisfying Stews & Chilis
Caramelized Onion Beef Stew • 19
Hearty Pork Stew • 20
Minestrone Stew • 21
Leek and Parsnip Vegetable Stew • 22
Family-Favorite Chili • 23
Buffalo Chicken Chili • 24
Black Bean–Sweet Potato Chili • 25

Metric Conversion Guide • 26
Recipe Testing and Calculating Nutrition
    Information • 27

Family Favorites

Beef and Potatoes with Rosemary

Prep Time: 20 Minutes • **Start to Finish:** 8 Hours 20 Minutes • Makes 8 servings

- 1 lb medium red potatoes, cut into quarters
- 1 cup ready-to-eat baby-cut carrots
- 3 tablespoons Dijon mustard
- 2 tablespoons chopped fresh or 1½ teaspoons dried rosemary leaves, crumbled
- 1 teaspoon chopped fresh or ½ teaspoon dried thyme leaves
- 1 teaspoon salt
- ½ teaspoon pepper
- 1 boneless beef chuck roast (3 lb), trimmed of excess fat
- 1 small onion, finely chopped (⅓ cup)
- 1½ cups beef broth (from 32-oz carton)

1 Spray 5- to 6-quart slow cooker with cooking spray. In slow cooker, place potatoes and carrots.

2 In small bowl, mix mustard, rosemary, thyme, salt and pepper; spread evenly over beef. Place beef on potatoes and carrots; sprinkle with onion. Pour broth evenly over beef and vegetables. Cover; cook on Low heat setting 8 to 10 hours or until beef and vegetables are tender.

3 Using slotted spoon, remove beef and vegetables from slow cooker; place on serving platter. Skim fat from beef juices if desired. Serve juices with beef and vegetables.

1 Serving: Calories 350; Total Fat 18g (Saturated Fat 7g, Trans Fat 1g); Cholesterol 95mg; Sodium 710mg; Total Carbohydrate 12g (Dietary Fiber 2g); Protein 33g **Exchanges:** ½ Starch, ½ Vegetable, 4½ Lean Meat, 1 Fat **Carbohydrate Choices:** 1

Beef and Potatoes with Rosemary and Gravy:
To make gravy, skim fat from juices in slow cooker. Measure 1½ cups of the juices; pour into small saucepan. Heat to boiling over medium-high heat. In tightly covered container, shake 2 tablespoons cornstarch and ¼ cup cold water. Stir cornstarch mixture into beef juices. Cook about 5 minutes, stirring occasionally, until thickened.

Tip Be sure to use red potatoes in this recipe. They will hold their shape better than russets.

Cheeseburger Joes

Prep Time: 20 Minutes • **Start to Finish:** 6 Hours 20 Minutes • Makes 12 sandwiches

- 1½ lb lean (at least 80%) ground beef
- ½ teaspoon garlic-pepper blend
- 1 loaf (8 oz) prepared cheese product, cut into small cubes (2 cups)
- 2 tablespoons milk
- 1 medium green bell pepper, chopped (1 cup)
- 1 small onion, chopped (⅓ cup)
- 2 cloves garlic, finely chopped
- 12 burger buns, split
- Sliced dill pickles, if desired

1 Spray 3½- to 4-quart slow cooker with cooking spray. In 12-inch skillet, cook beef and garlic-pepper blend over medium heat 8 to 10 minutes, stirring occasionally, until beef is thoroughly cooked; drain.

2 In slow cooker, mix beef, cheese, milk, bell pepper, onion and garlic.

3 Cover; cook on Low heat setting 6 to 7 hours. Stir. Serve beef mixture in buns with pickles.

1 Sandwich: Calories 280; Total Fat 13g (Saturated Fat 6g, Trans Fat 0.5g); Cholesterol 50mg; Sodium 520mg; Total Carbohydrate 21g (Dietary Fiber 1g); Protein 17g **Exchanges:** 1½ Starch, 2 Medium-Fat Meat **Carbohydrate Choices:** 1½

Porketta Pot Roast

Prep Time: 20 Minutes • **Start to Finish:** 9 Hours 20 Minutes • Makes 8 servings

- 2 teaspoons Italian seasoning
- 1½ teaspoons fennel seed, crushed
- ¾ teaspoon salt
- ½ teaspoon celery seed
- 1 boneless pork shoulder (3 lb), trimmed of fat
- 3 medium parsnips, peeled, cut into ¾-inch pieces (3 cups)
- 2 medium sweet potatoes, peeled, cut into ¾-inch pieces (3 cups)
- 12 cloves garlic, cut in half
- 1½ cups water

1 Spray 4- to 5-quart slow cooker with cooking spray. In small bowl, mix Italian seasoning, fennel seed, salt and celery seed. Pat seasoning mixture evenly onto pork (if pork comes in netting or is tied, do not remove). Heat 12-inch nonstick skillet over medium-high heat. Add pork; cook 5 to 10 minutes, turning several times, until brown on all sides.

2 In slow cooker, place parsnips, sweet potatoes and garlic; pour water over vegetables. Place pork on vegetables.

3 Cover; cook on Low heat setting 9 to 10 hours or until pork is tender.

4 Remove pork from slow cooker to cutting board (remove netting or strings). Cut pork across grain into slices. Serve with vegetables and cooking liquid.

1 Serving: Calories 350; Total Fat 20g (Saturated Fat 7g, Trans Fat 0g); Cholesterol 90mg; Sodium 290mg; Total Carbohydrate 16g (Dietary Fiber 3g); Protein 26g **Exchanges:** 1 Starch, 3 Medium-Fat Meat, 1 Fat **Carbohydrate Choices:** 1

Tip Parsnips go unnoticed among the more colorful, popular vegetables in the produce aisle. This delicious root vegetable looks like a thick white carrot with creamy-yellow to white flesh. When cooked, it is sweeter than a carrot. Parsnips are a source of iron and vitamin C.

Pulled Jerk Pork Sandwiches

Prep Time: 10 Minutes • **Start to Finish:** 8 Hours 40 Minutes • Makes 8 sandwiches

1 boneless pork shoulder (2½ lb), trimmed of fat
1 tablespoon Jamaican jerk seasoning (dry)
¼ teaspoon dried thyme leaves
1 medium onion, chopped (½ cup)
1 cup cola carbonated beverage
1¼ cups barbecue sauce
½ cup water
8 sandwich buns, split, or flour tortillas (8 to 10 inch)
Coleslaw, if desired

1 Spray 5- to 6-quart slow cooker with cooking spray. Rub pork with jerk seasoning and thyme (if pork comes in netting or is tied, do not remove). Place pork in slow cooker. Sprinkle with onion. Pour cola over top.

2 Cover; cook on Low heat setting 8 to 10 hours or until pork is tender.

3 Remove pork from slow cooker to cutting board (remove netting or strings). Remove cooking liquid and reserve. Shred pork with 2 forks; return to slow cooker. Stir in barbecue sauce, water and ½ cup of the reserved cooking liquid. Increase heat setting to High. Cover; cook 30 to 45 minutes or until heated through.

4 Spoon pork onto buns; top with coleslaw. In 2-quart saucepan, heat remaining cooking liquid to boiling; serve with sandwiches for dipping.

1 Sandwich Calories 340; Total Fat 7g (Saturated Fat 2g, Trans Fat 0g); Cholesterol 60mg; Sodium 710mg; Total Carbohydrate 36g (Dietary Fiber 3g); Protein 33g **Exchanges:** ½ Starch, 2 Other Carbohydrate, 3 Very Lean Meat, 1½ Lean Meat **Carbohydrate Choices:** 2½

Tip Pulled pork is a favorite style of Southern and some Southeastern barbecues. "Pulled" refers to the method of preparing the cooked pork by pulling it apart with your fingers or two forks.

Chicken and Vegetables with Dumplings

Prep Time: 10 Minutes • **Start to Finish:** 10 Hours • Makes 5 servings

2½ to 3 lb boneless skinless chicken thighs

1 lb small red potatoes (about 2½ inches in diameter)

1 medium onion, coarsely chopped (¾ cup)

2 cups baby-cut carrots

5¼ cups chicken broth (from two 32-oz cartons)

2 cups Original Bisquick® mix

½ cup water

2 teaspoons parsley flakes

1 In 5 to 6-quart slow cooker, place chicken, potatoes, onion and carrots. Add broth.

2 Cover; cook on Low heat setting 9 to 10 hours.

3 Increase heat setting to High. In medium bowl, stir together Bisquick mix, water and parsley. Drop dough by rounded tablespoonfuls onto hot chicken mixture. Cover; cook 45 to 50 minutes or until dumplings are dry in center.

1 Serving: Calories 680; Total Fat 26g (Saturated Fat 8g); Cholesterol 140mg; Sodium 1910mg; Total Carbohydrate 56g (Dietary Fiber 5g); Protein 59g
Exchanges: 1 Vegetable, 6 Lean Meat, 1 Fat **Carbohydrate Choices:** 4

Tip Serve this stew-type meal in a bowl with the broth. Add a tossed green salad garnished with grapefruit sections and drizzled with poppy seed dressing to this country-style dinner.

Tuscan Turkey and Beans

Prep Time: 30 Minutes • **Start to Finish:** 7 Hours 50 Minutes • Makes 6 servings

6 cups water
1 bag (16 oz) dried navy beans (2 cups), sorted, rinsed
3 cups chicken broth (from 32-oz carton)
¼ cup olive oil
¾ cup chopped parsley
1 tablespoon Italian seasoning
2 tablespoons chopped garlic
1½ teaspoons salt
½ teaspoon pepper
1 package (1½ to 2¼ lb) turkey thighs, skin removed
1½ cups frozen cut green beans, thawed

1 In 3-quart saucepan, heat water to boiling over medium-high heat. Add navy beans. Reduce heat to medium-low; simmer uncovered 10 minutes. Drain; rinse with cold water. Place beans in slow cooker; add broth.

2 Meanwhile, in medium bowl, stir together olive oil, ½ cup of the parsley, the Italian seasoning, garlic, ½ teaspoon of the salt and the pepper. Press mixture firmly onto turkey thighs. Place turkey on top of beans in slow cooker. Cover; cook on Low heat setting 7 to 9 hours or until beans are tender and turkey pulls apart easily with fork.

3 Remove turkey from slow cooker. Increase heat setting to High. Stir green beans and remaining 1 teaspoon salt into slow cooker. Cover; cook 15 to 20 minutes or until vegetables are hot. Meanwhile, remove turkey from bones. Place bean mixture in shallow bowls; top with turkey, and sprinkle with remaining parsley.

1 Serving: Calories 480; Total Fat 14g (Saturated Fat 2.5g, Trans Fat 0g); Cholesterol 90mg; Sodium 1080mg; Total Carbohydrate 49g (Dietary Fiber 19g); Protein 39g **Exchanges:** 2½ Starch, 2 Vegetable, 4 Lean Meat **Carbohydrate Choices:** 3

Tip This recipe would work equally well with pork or beef. Use a budget-friendly cut, such as pork shoulder or beef chuck roast.

Jambalaya

Prep Time: 20 Minutes • **Start to Finish:** 8 Hours 20 Minutes • Makes 8 servings

- 1 large onion, chopped (1 cup)
- 1 medium green bell pepper, chopped (1 cup)
- 2 medium stalks celery, chopped (1 cup)
- 3 cloves garlic, finely chopped
- 1 can (28 oz) diced tomatoes, undrained
- 2 cups chopped fully cooked smoked sausage
- 1 tablespoon parsley flakes
- ½ teaspoon dried thyme leaves
- ½ teaspoon salt
- ¼ teaspoon pepper
- ¼ teaspoon red pepper sauce
- ¾ lb uncooked deveined peeled medium shrimp, thawed if frozen, tail shells removed
- 3 cups uncooked regular long grain white rice

1 Spray 3½- to 6-quart slow cooker with cooking spray. In slow cooker, mix all ingredients except shrimp and rice. Cover; cook on Low heat setting 7 to 8 hours (or High heat setting 3 to 4 hours) or until vegetables are tender.

2 Stir in shrimp. Cover; cook about 1 hour longer or until shrimp are pink.

3 Cook rice as directed on package. Serve jambalaya with rice.

1 Serving: Calories 280; Total Fat 10g (Saturated Fat 3g, Trans Fat 0g); Cholesterol 90mg; Sodium 630mg; Total Carbohydrate 30g (Dietary Fiber 2g); Protein 16g **Exchanges:** 1½ Starch, 1½ Vegetable, 1 High-Fat Meat, ½ Fat **Carbohydrate Choices:** 2

Global Flavors

Chunky Beef Ragu

Prep Time: 35 Minutes • **Start to Finish:** 8 Hours 35 Minutes • Makes 6 servings

- 3 oz thinly sliced prosciutto or pancetta, chopped
- 1½ lb beef stew meat, cut into 1-inch pieces
- 2 jars (7 oz each) sun-dried tomatoes in oil, drained, chopped (1¼ cups)
- 2 medium carrots, sliced (1 cup)
- 1 cup chopped celery
- 1 medium onion, chopped (½ cup)
- 2 cloves garlic, finely chopped
- 1 can (14.5 oz) diced tomatoes, undrained
- ½ cup dry red wine
- 1½ teaspoons dried basil leaves
- 1½ teaspoons dried oregano leaves
- ½ teaspoon salt
- ¼ teaspoon crushed red pepper flakes

1 In 8-inch nonstick skillet, cook prosciutto over medium-high heat about 5 minutes, stirring frequently, until crisp. Drain on paper towels.

2 Spray 5- to 6-quart slow cooker with cooking spray. In slow cooker, mix prosciutto and remaining ingredients.

3 Cover; cook on Low heat setting 8 to 9 hours (or on High heat setting 4 hours to 4 hours 30 minutes).

1 Serving: Calories 300; Total Fat 16g (Saturated Fat 6g, Trans Fat 0.5g); Cholesterol 70mg; Sodium 640mg; Total Carbohydrate 13g (Dietary Fiber 3g); Protein 26g **Exchanges:** ½ Other Carbohydrate, 1 Vegetable, 3½ Lean Meat, 1 Fat **Carbohydrate Choices:** 1

Tip Serve your favorite pasta or mashed potatoes with this delicious dish.

Carnitas

Prep Time: 15 Minutes • **Start to Finish:** 4 Hours 15 Minutes • Makes 8 servings (2 tortillas each)

Carnitas

- 1 large sweet onion, sliced
- 1 tablespoon vegetable oil
- 1 package (1 oz) taco seasoning mix
- 1 boneless pork shoulder (3 lb)
- 1 can (10 oz) red enchilada sauce
- 1 can (4.5 oz) chopped green chiles, drained
- 16 flour tortillas for soft tacos and fajitas (6 inch)

Toppings, as desired

- ½ cup fresh cilantro leaves
- 1 cup shredded Cheddar cheese (4 oz)
- 1 cup sour cream

1 Spray 5- to 6-quart slow cooker with cooking spray; add onion.

2 In 10-inch nonstick skillet, heat oil over high heat. Sprinkle taco seasoning mix over pork shoulder, pressing to coat. Brown pork in oil on all sides; remove from skillet to slow cooker. Pour enchilada sauce over pork.

3 Cover; cook on High heat setting 4 to 5 hours or until tender. Remove pork from slow cooker; shred meat with fork. Place shredded pork in large bowl. Add chiles, 2 cups of the sauce from slow cooker and the onions; stir well.

4 Spoon pork mixture onto tortillas. Add toppings. Roll up tortillas.

1 Serving: Calories 530; Total Fat 27g (Saturated Fat 8g, Trans Fat 1.5g); Cholesterol 110mg; Sodium 1050mg; Total Carbohydrate 32g (Dietary Fiber 1g); Protein 40g **Exchanges:** 2 Starch, 2 Lean Meat, 3 Medium-Fat Meat, 1 Fat **Carbohydrate Choices:** 2

Tip Leftover carnitas filling is just as delicious the next day on tacos, in enchiladas, or even on pasta!

German Red Cabbage and Pork Ribs

Prep Time: 30 Minutes • **Start to Finish:** 5 Hours 30 Minutes • Makes 6 servings

4 slices bacon, chopped

6 boneless pork country-style ribs (2 lb)

1½ teaspoons salt

½ teaspoon pepper

6 cups thinly sliced red cabbage (about ½ head)

2 Granny Smith apples, peeled, thinly sliced (3 cups)

1 medium onion, finely chopped (½ cup)

½ cup cider vinegar

¼ cup apple juice

2 tablespoons sugar

1 In 12-inch skillet, cook bacon over medium-high heat, stirring occasionally, until crisp. Remove bacon from skillet to large bowl; reserve drippings in skillet. Sprinkle both sides of ribs with salt and pepper; cook in drippings until browned. Meanwhile, stir cabbage, apples and onion into bacon in bowl.

2 Spray 4- to 5-quart slow cooker with cooking spray. Place ribs in slow cooker, reserving drippings in skillet. Spoon cabbage mixture over ribs.

3 Stir vinegar, apple juice and sugar into drippings in skillet; heat to boiling. Pour over ribs and cabbage mixture.

4 Cover; cook on Low heat setting 5 to 6 hours. Use slotted spoon to remove cabbage mixture and ribs from cooker.

1 Serving: Calories 260; Total Fat 13g (Saturated Fat 4.5g, Trans Fat 0g); Cholesterol 50mg; Sodium 770mg; Total Carbohydrate 22g (Dietary Fiber 3g); Protein 13g **Exchanges:** 1 Other Carbohydrate, 1 Vegetable, 1½ Lean Meat, 2 Fat **Carbohydrate Choices:** 1½

Tip The slicing blade on a food processor does a quick job of shredding the cabbage. Cut the cabbage sections so they fit into the feed tube. To save time in the morning, slice the cabbage and chop the onion the night before, and refrigerate until needed.

Mediterranean Chicken Marbella

Prep Time: 15 Minutes • **Start to Finish:** 9 Hours 30 Minutes • Makes 8 servings

¼ cup packed brown sugar

2 teaspoons dried oregano leaves

1 teaspoon salt

¼ teaspoon pepper

3 cloves garlic, finely chopped

⅓ cup white wine or chicken broth

2 tablespoons red wine vinegar

2½ lb boneless skinless chicken thighs

2 dried bay leaves

½ cup pimiento-stuffed green olives

½ cup pitted bite-size prunes (from 12-oz package)

½ cup roasted red bell peppers (from 7-oz jar), drained, coarsely chopped

2 tablespoons capers, drained

1 box (10 oz) couscous

¼ cup chopped fresh parsley

1 In large bowl, mix brown sugar, oregano, salt, pepper, garlic, wine and vinegar. Add chicken; turn to coat well. Add bay leaves. Cover; refrigerate at least 4 hours or overnight to marinate.

2 Spray 3- to 4-quart slow cooker with cooking spray. In slow cooker, place chicken and marinade mixture.

3 Cover; cook on Low heat setting 5 to 6 hours.

4 Stir olives, prunes, roasted peppers and capers into chicken mixture in slow cooker. Cover; cook about 15 minutes longer or until hot. Meanwhile, cook couscous as directed on package.

5 Transfer chicken with juices to large serving bowl or deep platter; remove bay leaves. Sprinkle with parsley. Serve with couscous.

1 Serving: Calories 430; Total Fat 13g (Saturated Fat 4g, Trans Fat 0g); Cholesterol 85mg; Sodium 640mg; Total Carbohydrate 43g (Dietary Fiber 3g); Protein 35g **Exchanges:** 2 Starch, 1 Other Carbohydrate, 4 Lean Meat **Carbohydrate Choices:** 3

Tip You can skip the marinating step if you're short on time. Just mix all the ingredients from step 1 right in your slow cooker. The flavor will be a bit milder, but it's still delicious!

Spicy Chicken in Peanut Sauce

Prep Time: 15 Minutes • **Start to Finish:** 7 Hours 15 Minutes • Makes 4 servings

1 tablespoon olive or vegetable oil
8 large chicken thighs (about 3 lb), skin removed
1 large onion, chopped (1 cup)
2 cans (14.5 oz each) diced tomatoes with green chiles, undrained
1 can (14.5 oz) crushed tomatoes, undrained
2 tablespoons honey
1½ teaspoons ground cumin
1 teaspoon ground cinnamon
⅓ cup creamy peanut butter
2 cups hot cooked couscous

1 In 12-inch nonstick skillet, heat oil over medium-high heat. Cook chicken in oil about 4 minutes, turning once, until brown.

2 In 4- to 5-quart slow cooker, mix onion, diced and crushed tomatoes, honey, cumin and cinnamon. Add chicken. Spoon tomato mixture over chicken.

3 Cover; cook on Low heat setting 7 to 8 hours.

4 Stir in peanut butter until melted and well blended. Serve chicken and sauce over couscous.

1 Serving: Calories 740; Total Fat 33g (Saturated Fat 8g, Trans Fat 0.5g); Cholesterol 140mg; Sodium 1180mg; Total Carbohydrate 52g (Dietary Fiber 8g); Protein 60g **Exchanges:** 1 Starch, 1½ Other Carbohydrate, 3 Vegetable, 7½ Lean Meat, 2 Fat **Carbohydrate Choices:** 3½

Tip Pass small bowls of dry-roasted peanuts and chopped fresh cilantro to sprinkle over the chicken, and serve with wedges of warm pita bread.

Vegetable Curry with Couscous

Prep Time: 30 Minutes • **Start to Finish:** 5 Hours 40 Minutes • Makes 6 servings

Sauce

½ cup Yoplait Fat Free plain yogurt (from 32-oz container)

¼ cup chopped fresh cilantro leaves

1½ teaspoons lime juice

1 clove garlic, finely chopped

Dash salt

Dash freshly ground black pepper

Curry

2 teaspoons vegetable oil

½ cup chopped onion (1 medium)

2 cloves garlic, finely chopped

2 teaspoons curry powder

½ teaspoon ground turmeric

¼ teaspoon ground cinnamon

⅛ teaspoon ground red pepper (cayenne)

3 cups cubed (¾ to 1 inch) peeled eggplant

2 medium tomatoes, coarsely chopped (1 cup)

1 medium red bell pepper, coarsely chopped (1 cup)

1 cup sliced (¼ inch) ready-to-eat baby-cut carrots

1 can (15 oz) chick peas (garbanzo beans), drained

½ teaspoon salt

¼ teaspoon pepper

2 cups fresh baby spinach leaves

2 cups uncooked whole wheat couscous

1 In medium bowl, mix all sauce ingredients. Refrigerate until serving time.

2 In 10-inch nonstick skillet, heat oil over medium heat. Add onion; cook about 5 minutes, stirring occasionally, until translucent. Add garlic; cook, stirring frequently, until softened. Stir in curry powder, turmeric, cinnamon and red pepper; cook and stir about 30 seconds.

3 Spray 3- or 4-quart slow cooker with cooking spray. In cooker, mix onion mixture and all remaining curry ingredients except spinach and couscous.

4 Cover; cook on Low heat setting 5 to 6 hours.

5 Stir spinach into curry in cooker. Cover; cook on Low heat setting 5 to 10 minutes longer or until slightly wilted.

6 Meanwhile, cook couscous as directed on package. Serve curry over couscous; top with sauce.

1 Serving: Calories 370; Total Fat 4.5g (Saturated Fat 0.5g, Trans Fat 0g); Cholesterol 0mg; Sodium 350mg; Total Carbohydrate 67g (Dietary Fiber 11g); Protein 14g **Exchanges:** 3 Starch, 1 Other Carbohydrate, 2 Vegetable, ½ Fat **Carbohydrate Choices:** 4½

Tip If you can't find whole wheat couscous at your grocery store, use the more traditional couscous instead.

Satisfying Stews & Chilis

Caramelized Onion Beef Stew

Prep Time: 35 Minutes • **Start to Finish:** 8 Hours 50 Minutes • Makes 6 servings

- 2 tablespoons butter or margarine
- 4 cups halved and thinly sliced sweet onions (about 1½ onions)
- 2 teaspoons sugar
- 2 teaspoons chopped fresh thyme leaves
- 1½ lb beef stew meat
- 1 cup beef broth (from 32-oz carton)
- 1 package (.87 oz) onion gravy mix
- 2 cups 1-inch pieces diagonally cut carrots
- 1 cup 1-inch pieces diagonally cut parsnips
- ½ cup frozen sweet peas

1 In 10-inch skillet, melt butter over medium-low heat. Cook onions and sugar in butter 30 to 35 minutes, stirring frequently, until onions are deep golden brown and caramelized. Stir in thyme and stew meat; place in slow cooker.

2 In medium bowl, mix broth and gravy mix; pour over meat mixture in slow cooker. Top with carrots and parsnips. Cover; cook on Low heat setting 8 to 9 hours or until beef and vegetables are tender.

3 Stir in peas. Cover; cook 10 to 15 minutes longer or until hot.

1 Serving: Calories 290; Total Fat 15g (Saturated Fat 6g, Trans Fat 0.5g); Cholesterol 60mg; Sodium 450mg; Total Carbohydrate 21g (Dietary Fiber 4g); Protein 18g **Exchanges:** 1 Starch, 1 Vegetable, 2 Lean Meat, 1½ Fat **Carbohydrate Choices:** 1½

Tip Serve this saucy beef stew over mashed potatoes with plenty of crusty bread for soaking up the extra sauce.

Hearty Pork Stew

Prep Time: 25 Minutes • **Start to Finish:** 7 Hours 10 Minutes • Makes 6 servings

- 1½ lb boneless pork loin, cut into 1-inch cubes
- 2 cups diced (½ inch) peeled parsnips (3 medium)
- 1½ cups cubed (1 inch) peeled butternut squash
- 3 medium carrots, cut into ¼-inch slices (1½ cups)
- 1 medium onion, chopped (½ cup)
- 1 carton (32 oz) chicken broth (4 cups)
- ½ teaspoon salt
- ½ teaspoon pepper
- 3 tablespoons Gold Medal® all-purpose flour
- 3 tablespoons butter, softened

1 Spray 3½- to 6-quart slow cooker with cooking spray. In slow cooker, mix all ingredients except flour and butter.

2 Cover; cook on Low heat setting 6 to 7 hours (or on High heat setting 3 to 4 hours) or until pork is no longer pink and vegetables are tender.

3 In small bowl, mix flour and butter; gently stir into pork mixture, one spoonful at a time, until blended. If using Low heat setting, increase to High. Cover; cook 30 to 45 minutes longer, stirring occasionally, until thickened.

1 Serving: Calories 290; Total Fat 11g (Saturated Fat 5g, Trans Fat 0g); Cholesterol 65mg; Sodium 960mg; Total Carbohydrate 19g (Dietary Fiber 4g); Protein 27g **Exchanges:** 1 Starch, 1 Vegetable, 3 Lean Meat, ½ Fat **Carbohydrate Choices:** 1

Minestrone Stew

Prep Time: 15 Minutes • **Start to Finish:** 6 Hours 35 Minutes • Makes 8 servings

- 1 package (19.5 oz) gluten-free sweet Italian turkey sausage links, casings removed
- 1 can (28 oz) diced tomatoes, undrained
- 2 cans (18 oz each) garden vegetable soup
- 1 can (15 oz) garbanzo beans, drained, rinsed
- 1 can (6 oz) tomato paste
- 1 teaspoon gluten-free Italian seasoning
- 1 cup uncooked gluten-free elbow macaroni (about 4 oz)
- ½ cup gluten-free shredded Parmesan cheese (2 oz)

1 In 12-inch skillet, cook sausage over medium heat 8 to 10 minutes, stirring occasionally, until no longer pink; drain. Spray 3- to 4-quart slow cooker with cooking spray. In slow cooker, mix sausage and all remaining ingredients except macaroni and cheese.

2 Cover; cook on Low heat setting 6 hours.

3 Stir macaroni into slow cooker. Increase heat setting to High. Cover; cook about 20 minutes longer or until macaroni is tender. Sprinkle with cheese.

1 Serving: Calories 330; Total Fat 10g (Saturated Fat 3g, Trans Fat 0g); Cholesterol 45mg; Sodium 1190mg; Total Carbohydrate 38g (Dietary Fiber 6g); Protein 20g **Exchanges:** ½ Starch, 1½ Other Carbohydrate, 1½ Vegetable, 1 Very Lean Meat, 1½ Lean Meat, 1 Fat **Carbohydrate Choices:** 2½

Tip Cooking gluten free? Always read labels to make sure each recipe ingredient is gluten free. Products and ingredient sources can change.

Leek and Parsnip Vegetable Stew

Prep Time: 20 Minutes • **Start to Finish:** 8 Hours 40 Minutes • Makes 8 servings

- 4 medium red potatoes, cut into ½-inch pieces
- 2 medium leeks, rinsed, cut in half lengthwise and sliced into ½-inch pieces (4 cups)
- 4 medium stalks celery, cut into ½-inch pieces (2 cups)
- 3 medium carrots, cut into ½-inch pieces (1½ cups)
- 2 medium parsnips, peeled, cut into ½-inch pieces (1½ cups)
- 1 can (28 oz) whole tomatoes, undrained, cut up
- 1 can (14 oz) vegetable broth
- ½ teaspoon dried thyme leaves
- ½ teaspoon dried rosemary leaves
- ½ teaspoon salt
- 3 tablespoons cornstarch
- 3 tablespoons cold water

1 Spray 4- to 5-quart slow cooker with cooking spray. In slow cooker, mix all ingredients except cornstarch and water. Cover; cook on Low heat setting 8 to 10 hours.

2 In small bowl, mix cornstarch and water until smooth; gradually stir into stew until blended. Increase heat setting to High. Cover; cook about 20 minutes longer, stirring occasionally, until thickened.

1 Serving: Calories 170; Total Fat 0g (Saturated Fat 0g, Trans Fat 0g); Cholesterol 0mg; Sodium 550mg; Total Carbohydrate 39g (Dietary Fiber 6g); Protein 3g **Exchanges:** 2 Other Carbohydrate, 2 Vegetable **Carbohydrate Choices:** 2½

Tip Parsnips, a root vegetable that looks like creamy white carrots, have a slightly sweet flavor. If you don't have any on hand, you can use carrots instead.

Family-Favorite Chili

Prep Time: 20 Minutes • **Start to Finish:** 6 Hours 35 Minutes • Makes 8 servings

- 2 lb lean (at least 80%) ground beef
- 1 large onion, chopped (1 cup)
- 2 cloves garlic, finely chopped
- 1 can (28 oz) diced tomatoes, undrained
- 1 can (15 oz) tomato sauce
- 2 tablespoons chili powder
- 1½ teaspoons ground cumin
- ½ teaspoon salt
- ½ teaspoon pepper
- 1 can (15 to 16 oz) kidney or pinto beans, drained, rinsed
- Shredded Cheddar cheese, if desired

1 In 12-inch skillet, cook beef over medium heat 8 to 10 minutes, stirring occasionally, until brown; drain.

2 Spray 3½- to 6-quart slow cooker with cooking spray. In slow cooker, mix beef and all remaining ingredients except beans and cheese. Cover; cook on Low heat setting 6 to 8 hours (or High heat setting 3 to 4 hours).

3 Stir in beans. Increase heat setting to High. Cover; cook 15 to 20 minutes longer or until slightly thickened. Sprinkle with cheese.

1 Serving: Calories 300; Total Fat 12g (Saturated Fat 4.5g, Trans Fat 0.5g); Cholesterol 70mg; Sodium 800mg; Total Carbohydrate 22g (Dietary Fiber 6g); Protein 27g **Exchanges:** 1 Starch, 1 Vegetable, 3½ Lean Meat **Carbohydrate Choices:** 1½

Family-Favorite Chili with Smoked Sausage:
Reduce ground beef to 1 lb. Add 1 lb cooked smoked beef sausage, cut into ½-inch slices, in step 2. Substitute shredded smoked Cheddar or smoked Gouda cheese for the shredded Cheddar.

Family-Favorite Turkey Chili with Brown Rice:
Substitute ground turkey breast for the ground beef, cooking until no longer pink in step 1. Serve chili over cooked brown rice. Substitute shredded reduced-fat Cheddar cheese for the shredded Cheddar.

Buffalo Chicken Chili

Prep Time: 15 Minutes • **Start to Finish:** 8 Hours 15 Minutes • Makes 6 servings

- 2½ lb boneless skinless chicken thighs, cut into 1-inch pieces
- 1 large onion, chopped (1 cup)
- 2 medium stalks celery, sliced (1 cup)
- 2 medium carrots, chopped (1 cup)
- 1 can (28 oz) diced tomatoes, undrained
- 1 can (15 oz) black beans, drained, rinsed
- 1 cup chicken broth (from 32-oz carton)
- 2 teaspoons chili powder
- ½ teaspoon salt
- ¼ cup Buffalo wing sauce
- Crumbled blue cheese, if desired

1 Spray 5- to 6-quart slow cooker with cooking spray. In slow cooker, mix all ingredients except Buffalo wing sauce and cheese.

2 Cover; cook on Low heat setting 8 to 10 hours.

3 Stir in Buffalo wing sauce. Sprinkle individual servings with cheese.

1 Serving: Calories 430; Total Fat 16g (Saturated Fat 5g, Trans Fat 0g); Cholesterol 115mg; Sodium 920mg; Total Carbohydrate 27g (Dietary Fiber 9g); Protein 46g **Exchanges:** 1 Starch, ½ Other Carbohydrate, 1 Vegetable, 6 Very Lean Meat, 2 Fat **Carbohydrate Choices:** 2

Tip If you don't have Buffalo wing sauce, you can use a mixture of ½ teaspoon red pepper sauce and ¼ teaspoon ground red pepper (cayenne).

Black Bean–Sweet Potato Chili

Prep Time: 35 Minutes • **Start to Finish:** 7 Hours 35 Minutes • Makes 8 servings

- 2 large dark-orange sweet potatoes (1½ lb), peeled, cut into ½-inch cubes (about 5 cups)
- 3 large onions, chopped (3 cups)
- 3 cloves garlic, finely chopped
- 2 tablespoons chili powder
- 1 tablespoon ground cumin
- 1 can (28 oz) diced tomatoes, undrained
- 1 can (16 oz) refried black beans
- 1 can (15 oz) black beans, drained, rinsed
- 2 cups chicken broth (from 32-oz carton)
- 2 teaspoons red wine vinegar
- Shredded cheese, if desired
- Sour cream, if desired

1 Spray 5- to 6-quart slow cooker with cooking spray. In slow cooker, mix all ingredients except vinegar, cheese and sour cream.

2 Cover; cook on Low heat setting 7 to 8 hours (or on High heat setting 3 hours 30 minutes to 4 hours).

3 Stir in vinegar. Serve chili with cheese and sour cream.

1 Serving: Calories 260; Total Fat 2g (Saturated Fat 0.5g, Trans Fat 0g); Cholesterol 0mg; Sodium 900mg; Total Carbohydrate 48g (Dietary Fiber 13g); Protein 12g **Exchanges:** 2½ Other Carbohydrate, 2 Vegetable, 1 Lean Meat **Carbohydrate Choices:** 3

Tip Make quick work of chopping the garlic and onions by enlisting the help of your food processor. Start by chopping the garlic first, then add the onions and continue chopping. Depending on the size of your food processor, you may need to do the onions in batches. Either way, you save time and tears!

Metric Conversion Guide

Volume

U.S. Units	Canadian Metric	Australian Metric
¼ teaspoon	1 mL	1 ml
½ teaspoon	2 mL	2 ml
1 teaspoon	5 mL	5 ml
1 tablespoon	15 mL	20 ml
¼ cup	50 mL	60 ml
⅓ cup	75 mL	80 ml
½ cup	125 mL	125 ml
⅔ cup	150 mL	170 ml
¾ cup	175 mL	190 ml
1 cup	250 mL	250 ml
1 quart	1 liter	1 liter
1½ quarts	1.5 liters	1.5 liters
2 quarts	2 liters	2 liters
2½ quarts	2.5 liters	2.5 liters
3 quarts	3 liters	3 liters
4 quarts	4 liters	4 liters

Weight

U.S. Units	Canadian Metric	Australian Metric
1 ounce	30 grams	30 grams
2 ounces	55 grams	60 grams
3 ounces	85 grams	90 grams
4 ounces (¼ pound)	115 grams	125 grams
8 ounces (½ pound)	225 grams	225 grams
16 ounces (1 pound)	455 grams	500 grams
1 pound	455 grams	0.5 kilogram

Note: The recipes in this cookbook have not been developed or tested using metric measures. When converting recipes to metric, some variations in quality may be noted.

Measurements

Inches	Centimeters
1	2.5
2	5.0
3	7.5
4	10.0
5	12.5
6	15.0
7	17.5
8	20.5
9	23.0
10	25.5
11	28.0
12	30.5
13	33.0

Temperatures

Fahrenheit	Celsius
32°	0°
212°	100°
250°	120°
275°	140°
300°	150°
325°	160°
350°	180°
375°	190°
400°	200°
425°	220°
450°	230°
475°	240°
500°	260°

Recipe Testing and Calculating Nutrition Information

Recipe Testing:

- Large eggs and 2% milk were used unless otherwise indicated.
- Fat-free, low-fat, low-sodium or lite products were not used unless indicated.
- No nonstick cookware and bakeware were used unless otherwise indicated. No dark-colored, black or insulated bakeware was used.
- When a pan is specified, a metal pan was used; a baking dish or pie plate means ovenproof glass was used.
- An electric hand mixer was used for mixing only when mixer speeds are specified.

Calculating Nutrition:

- The first ingredient was used wherever a choice is given, such as ⅓ cup sour cream or plain yogurt.
- The first amount was used wherever a range is given, such as 3- to 3½-pound whole chicken.
- The first serving number was used wherever a range is given, such as 4 to 6 servings.
- "If desired" ingredients were not included.
- Only the amount of a marinade or frying oil that is absorbed was included.

America's most trusted cookbook is better than ever!

- 1,100 all-new photos, including hundreds of step-by-step images
- More than 1,500 recipes, with hundreds of inspiring variations and creative "mini" recipes for easy cooking ideas
- Brand-new features
- Gorgeous new design

Get the best edition of the *Betty Crocker Cookbook* today!

www.ingramcontent.com/pod-product-compliance
Lightning Source LLC
Chambersburg PA
CBHW071418290426
44108CB00014B/1882